Back to Work: Navigating Job Gaps for Career Success © 2024 Marie Rose Penn

All rights reserved.

No part of this book may be reproduced, distributed, or transmitted in any form or by any means, including photocopying, recording, or other electronic or mechanical methods, without the prior written permission of the publisher, except in the case of brief quotations embodied in critical reviews and certain other non-commercial uses permitted by copyright law.

Cover Design: Marie Rose Penn

Marie Rose Penn

Back to Work

Navigating Job Gaps for Career Success

Contents

Introduction	1
Chapter 1 Understanding Employment Gaps	8
Chapter 2 Overcoming the Stigma of Employment Gaps	29
Chapter 3 Strategies for Re-Entering the Workforce	54
Chapter 4 Crafting Your Winning Resume	67
Chapter 5 Acing the Interview	83
Chapter 6 Mindset and Mental Health	99
Chapter 7 Daily Routines for Success	112

Chapter 8   125
Continuous Learning and Skill Development

Chapter 9   139
Real-Life Success Stories

Your Path to Career Triumph: 173
Final Thoughts

Appendices   186
Appendix A: Sample Resumes and Cover Letters   186
Appendix B: Helpful Resources   198
Appendix C: Interview Preparation Tools   203
Appendix D: Sample Interview Questions and Answers   205
Appendix E: Resource List   210

Final Note   219

Introduction

In today's dynamic and ever-changing job market, periods of unemployment are more common than ever before. Whether due to economic downturns, personal health challenges, caregiving responsibilities, or voluntary career breaks, many of us will face employment gaps at some point in our careers. These gaps, while often daunting, do not define our professional worth or potential for future success. Instead, they can serve as opportunities for growth, reflection, and reinvention.

This book, "Navigating Job Gaps for Career Success," is designed to be your comprehensive guide through the complex terrain of employment gaps. It provides practical strategies, insightful advice, and real-life success stories to help you turn these periods of uncertainty into powerful stepping stones toward achieving your career goals.

Why This Book Matters

Understanding how to navigate employment gaps is crucial for anyone looking to re-enter the workforce with confidence and resilience. This book addresses the stigma often associated with job gaps and offers actionable solutions to overcome these challenges. By embracing a positive mindset and employing effective strategies, you can transform potential obstacles into opportunities for personal and professional growth.

What You'll Learn

Throughout the chapters, you will discover a wealth of information tailored to help you succeed in your job search and career development. Here's a glimpse of what you can expect:

- **Chapter 1: Understanding Employment Gaps**: Gain insights into the common reasons for employment gaps and how to address them effectively with potential employers.

- **Chapter 2: Overcoming the Stigma of Employment Gaps**: Learn strategies to change perspectives on job gaps and turn them into strengths.

- **Chapter 3: Strategies for Re-Entering the Workforce**: Explore networking, social media, volunteering, freelancing, and part-time work as avenues to bridge employment gaps.

- **Chapter 4: Crafting Your Winning Resume**: Create a compelling resume that highlights your strengths and minimizes the impact of employment gaps.

- **Chapter 5: Acing the Interview**: Prepare for interviews with confidence, addressing employment gaps positively and making a strong impression on employers.

- **Chapter 6: Mindset and Mental Health**: Manage anxiety, depression, and low self-esteem while building confidence and maintaining a positive outlook.

- **Chapter 7: Daily Routines for Success**: Establish effective daily routines and maintain a healthy lifestyle to stay productive and focused.

- **Chapter 8: Continuous Learning and Skill Development**: Embrace lifelong learning to stay competitive and achieve long-term career success.

- **Chapter 9: Real-Life Success Stories**: Draw inspiration from individuals who have successfully navigated employment gaps and achieved their career goals.

A Journey of Resilience and Growth

Navigating employment gaps requires resilience, adaptability, and a willingness to learn and grow. This book is more than a guide; it's a companion on your journey to career success. It empowers you to take control of your career narrative, leverage your unique experiences, and present yourself as a strong and capable candidate.

As you embark on this journey, remember that you are not alone. Many others have faced similar challenges and emerged stronger and more determined. With the right mindset, strategies, and support, you too can turn employment gaps into opportunities for a fulfilling and successful career.

Welcome to "Navigating Job Gaps for Career Success." Let's begin this transformative journey together.

Chapter 1
Understanding Employment Gaps

In today's ever-evolving job market, employment gaps have become increasingly common. Whether due to layoffs, voluntary career breaks, health issues, or caregiving responsibilities, many individuals find themselves with periods of unemployment. While these gaps can feel daunting, they are not insurmountable barriers. This chapter aims to demystify employment gaps, explain why they might raise concerns for employers, and provide insights into addressing these concerns effectively.

The Reality of Employment Gaps

Employment gaps occur when an individual is out of work for an extended period. These gaps can be the result of various life circumstances, such as:

- **Layoffs**: Companies downsize, restructure, or close operations, leading to job losses.
- **Voluntary Breaks**: Individuals may take time off to travel, pursue further education, or reassess their career paths.
- **Health Issues**: Physical or mental health challenges can necessitate a break from work.
- **Family Responsibilities**: Caring for children, elderly parents, or other family members can require time away from the workforce.

- **Economic Conditions**: Recessions and economic downturns can lead to prolonged periods of joblessness.

These situations are part of life, and many people experience them at some point in their careers. However, they can pose challenges when re-entering the job market.

Employer Concerns

Employers often have reservations about hiring individuals with employment gaps. These concerns can stem from a variety of factors:

- **Skill Atrophy**: Employers may worry that prolonged unemployment has led to outdated skills.

- **Commitment**: Questions about an individual's dedication and reliability might arise, especially if the reasons for the gap are not clearly explained.
- **Performance Issues**: Employers might wonder if the gap was due to performance-related problems in previous roles.
- **Adaptability**: Concerns about an individual's ability to adapt to new workplace technologies and methodologies may be a factor.

Understanding these concerns is crucial to addressing them effectively. Being prepared to discuss employment gaps candidly and positively can help alleviate employer apprehensions.

Changing Perspectives on Employment Gaps

The modern job market is beginning to recognize that career breaks do not necessarily reflect negatively on a candidate's abilities or potential. In fact, many employers are becoming more open to the idea that employment gaps can contribute to a candidate's overall growth and resilience. This shift in perspective is partly due to:

- **Increased Awareness**: Greater awareness of mental health, work-life balance, and the importance of personal growth.
- **Diverse Work Histories**: The rise of gig work, freelance opportunities, and remote work has led to more varied career paths.

- **Focus on Skills**: Employers are placing greater emphasis on skills and competencies rather than continuous employment history.

By leveraging these changes, candidates can reframe their employment gaps as periods of growth, learning, and development.

Addressing Employment Gaps Head-On

One of the most effective ways to mitigate concerns about employment gaps is to address them directly in resumes, cover letters, and interviews. Here are some strategies to consider:

1. Be Honest and Transparent

- **Resume**: Briefly mention the gap in your employment history and

provide a concise explanation. For example, "Career break for health reasons (2019-2020)" or "Maternity leave (2020-2021)."
- **Cover Letter**: Use the cover letter to expand on the gap and highlight any relevant activities or skills acquired during this period.
- **Interview**: Be prepared to discuss the gap confidently and positively. Focus on what you learned and how you stayed engaged with your field.

2. Highlight Relevant Activities During the Gap

- **Volunteer Work**: Mention any volunteer work, pro bono projects, or community involvement. These activities demonstrate commitment and a proactive approach.

- **Freelancing and Consulting**: If you took on freelance or consulting work during the gap, highlight these experiences and the skills you developed.
- **Education and Skill Development**: Emphasize any courses, certifications, or training you completed during the gap.

3. Focus on Transferable Skills

- Highlight skills that are relevant to the job you are applying for, even if they were acquired during your employment gap. For example, project management skills gained through organizing community events or technical skills developed through online courses.

4. Provide Strong References

- Obtain references from individuals who can vouch for your abilities and character during your employment gap. This could be a volunteer coordinator, a freelance client, or an instructor from a course you completed.

Real-Life Example

Consider the case of Sarah, a marketing professional who took a two-year career break to care for her elderly parents. During this time, Sarah stayed active in her field by:

- Volunteering as a marketing coordinator for a local non-profit organization.

- Completing a digital marketing certification course.
- Freelancing for small businesses, helping them develop social media strategies.

When Sarah decided to re-enter the workforce, she addressed her employment gap head-on in her resume and cover letter. In her resume, she included a brief mention of her caregiving responsibilities and highlighted her volunteer and freelance work. In her cover letter, she explained her career break and emphasized the skills and experiences she gained during this period. During interviews, Sarah confidently discussed her gap and provided strong references from her volunteer and freelance work. As a result, she successfully landed a job as a marketing manager at a reputable company.

Strategies for Addressing Employment Gaps

To effectively address employment gaps, it's important to employ a combination of transparency, skill development, and strategic presentation. Here are some practical strategies to consider:

1. Reframe the Narrative

- **Positive Framing**: Turn the gap into a story of growth and resilience. Instead of viewing it as a setback, present it as a time when you developed new skills, gained valuable experiences, or made significant contributions through volunteer work.

- **Focus on Achievements**: Highlight any accomplishments during the gap, such as certifications earned, courses completed, or volunteer projects led.

2. Continuous Learning and Skill Development

- **Online Courses and Certifications**: Utilize platforms like Coursera, LinkedIn Learning, and Udemy to keep your skills up-to-date and demonstrate your commitment to continuous learning.
- **Workshops and Seminars**: Attend industry-related workshops, webinars, and seminars to stay connected with your field and expand your knowledge base.

- **Networking Events**: Participate in networking events, both in-person and virtual, to meet industry professionals and stay informed about trends and opportunities.

3. Freelancing and Consulting

- **Short-Term Projects**: Take on freelance or consulting projects related to your field. This not only helps you maintain your skills but also provides valuable experience that can be showcased on your resume.
- **Building a Portfolio**: Create a portfolio of your freelance work to demonstrate your expertise and accomplishments to potential employers.

4. Volunteering and Pro Bono Work

- **Community Involvement**: Engage in volunteer work or pro bono projects that align with your career interests. This not only fills employment gaps but also demonstrates your commitment and willingness to contribute.
- **Leadership Roles**: Take on leadership roles in volunteer organizations or community projects to showcase your ability to manage teams and drive initiatives.
- **References from Volunteer Work**: Obtain references from volunteer coordinators or project leads who can vouch for your skills and dedication.

Addressing Employment Gaps in Different Contexts

Employment gaps can arise from various situations, each with its own set of challenges and strategies for addressing them. Here are some common scenarios and tips for navigating them:

1. Layoffs and Redundancies
- **Be Honest About the Situation**: Explain the circumstances of the layoff or redundancy in a straightforward manner. Emphasize that it was due to factors beyond your control, such as company restructuring or economic downturns.
- **Highlight Your Contributions**: Focus on your accomplishments and contributions during your time with

the previous employer. Mention any positive feedback or performance reviews you received.

2. Career Breaks for Personal Reasons

- **Explain the Reason Briefly**: Provide a brief explanation for the career break, such as personal health issues, family responsibilities, or travel. Keep the explanation concise and professional.
- **Focus on Skills Gained**: Emphasize any skills or experiences you gained during the break that are relevant to the job you are applying for. For example, if you took a break to care for a family member, highlight your time

management, multitasking, and problem-solving skills.

3. Long-Term Illness or Disability

- **Address Health Issues Tactfully**: If you took a break due to health issues, provide a concise explanation without going into too much detail. Reassure potential employers that your health has improved and that you are fully capable of performing the job.
- **Emphasize Resilience and Adaptability**: Highlight how you have adapted to challenges and demonstrated resilience during your recovery. Mention any new skills or knowledge you acquired during this time.

4. Maternity or Parental Leave
- **Acknowledge the Career Break**: Mention the career break for maternity or parental leave in a straightforward manner. Emphasize that it was an important and fulfilling period of your life.
- **Highlight Transferable Skills**: Focus on skills gained during this period, such as multitasking, time management, and organizational skills. These are valuable traits that can benefit any workplace.

Embracing a Growth Mindset

A growth mindset is the belief that abilities and intelligence can be developed through dedication and hard work. Embracing this mindset can help you navigate employment gaps more effectively and present yourself as a resilient and adaptable candidate. Here are some ways to cultivate a growth mindset:

1. Embrace Challenges
- **View Challenges as Opportunities**: Instead of avoiding challenges, see them as opportunities to learn and grow. Each challenge you face can help you develop new skills and gain valuable experiences.

2. Learn from Feedback
- **Seek Constructive Criticism**: Actively seek feedback from mentors, colleagues, and peers. Use this feedback to improve your skills and performance.

- **Reflect on Mistakes**: View mistakes as learning opportunities. Reflect on what went wrong and how you can improve in the future.

3. Set Realistic Goals

- **Short-Term and Long-Term Goals**: Set both short-term and long-term goals to guide your career development. Break these goals into manageable steps and celebrate your progress along the way.
- **Focus on Continuous Improvement**: Strive for continuous improvement in all areas of your life. Whether it's learning a new skill or enhancing your existing ones, commit to ongoing development.

Conclusion

Understanding and addressing employment gaps is a crucial step in re-entering the workforce. By reframing the narrative, engaging in continuous learning, leveraging freelance and volunteer opportunities, and embracing a growth mindset, you can turn employment gaps into valuable experiences that enhance your career prospects. Employers are increasingly recognizing the diverse paths individuals take in their careers, and with the right strategies, you can confidently navigate the job market and achieve your career goals.

Chapter 2
Overcoming the Stigma of Employment Gaps

Employment gaps can be a source of anxiety for many job seekers, as they worry about how these gaps will be perceived by potential employers. However, the stigma associated with employment gaps is gradually fading as more people experience breaks in their careers for various reasons. In this chapter, we will explore strategies for changing perspectives on employment gaps, addressing concerns head-on, and turning these gaps into strengths during job searches.

Changing Perspectives on Employment Gaps

The modern workforce is evolving, and with it, the understanding of non-linear career paths. Several factors contribute to a more accepting view of employment gaps:

1. Increased Awareness of Mental Health and Work-Life Balance

- **Mental Health Awareness**: Society's growing recognition of mental health issues has led to a better understanding of the need for breaks to address personal well-being.
- **Work-Life Balance**: Employers are increasingly valuing employees who prioritize a healthy work-life balance, recognizing that this leads

to happier and more productive team members.

2. Diverse Work Histories

- **Gig Economy and Freelancing**: The rise of gig work and freelancing has created a more varied approach to careers. Short-term contracts, project-based work, and freelance opportunities are now common, making employment gaps less significant.
- **Career Changes**: With the fast pace of technological and industrial change, career shifts are becoming more common. It is normal for people to take breaks to reskill or pivot to new industries.

3. Focus on Skills and Competencies

- **Skills Over Tenure**: Many employers now prioritize skills and competencies over continuous employment history. They seek candidates who can demonstrate the ability to learn and adapt quickly.
- **Transferable Skills**: Skills gained during employment gaps, such as project management, leadership, or technical skills, are often highly valuable to employers.

Addressing Employment Gaps Directly

To effectively address employment gaps, it is essential to be proactive and transparent. Here are some strategies to help:

1. **Be Honest and Transparent**
   - **Resume**: Briefly mention the gap in your employment history and provide a concise explanation, such as "Career break for health reasons (2019-2020)" or "Maternity leave (2020-2021)."
   - **Cover Letter**: Use the cover letter to expand on the gap and highlight any relevant activities or skills acquired during this period.
   - **Interview**: Be prepared to discuss the gap confidently and positively. Focus on what you learned and how you stayed engaged with your field.

2. **Highlight Relevant Activities During the Gap**
   - **Volunteer Work**: Mention any volunteer work, pro bono projects, or community involvement. These

activities demonstrate commitment and a proactive approach.

- **Freelancing and Consulting**: If you took on freelance or consulting work during the gap, highlight these experiences and the skills you developed.
- **Education and Skill Development**: Emphasize any courses, certifications, or training you completed during the gap.

3. Focus on Transferable Skills

- Highlight skills that are relevant to the job you are applying for, even if they were acquired during your employment gap. For example, project management skills gained through organizing community events or technical skills developed through online courses.

4. Provide Strong References
- Obtain references from individuals who can vouch for your abilities and character during your employment gap. This could be a volunteer coordinator, a freelance client, or an instructor from a course you completed.

Turning Employment Gaps into Strengths

With the right approach, employment gaps can be reframed as periods of growth and opportunity. Here are some ways to turn these gaps into strengths:

1. Reframe the Narrative
- **Positive Framing**: Present the gap as a time of personal and professional development. Highlight

the new skills, experiences, and perspectives you gained during this period.
- **Focus on Achievements**: Emphasize any accomplishments during the gap, such as certifications earned, courses completed, or volunteer projects led.

2. **Continuous Learning and Skill Development**
    - **Online Courses and Certifications**: Utilize platforms like Coursera, LinkedIn Learning, and Udemy to keep your skills up-to-date and demonstrate your commitment to continuous learning.
    - **Workshops and Seminars**: Attend industry-related workshops,

webinars, and seminars to stay connected with your field and expand your knowledge base.
- **Networking Events**: Participate in networking events, both in-person and virtual, to meet industry professionals and stay informed about trends and opportunities.

3. **Freelancing and Consulting**
   - **Short-Term Projects**: Take on freelance or consulting projects related to your field. This not only helps you maintain your skills but also provides valuable experience that can be showcased on your resume.
   - **Building a Portfolio**: Create a portfolio of your freelance work to demonstrate your expertise and

accomplishments to potential employers.

4. Volunteering and Pro Bono Work

- **Community Involvement**: Engage in volunteer work or pro bono projects that align with your career interests. This not only fills employment gaps but also demonstrates your commitment and willingness to contribute.
- **Leadership Roles**: Take on leadership roles in volunteer organizations or community projects to showcase your ability to manage teams and drive initiatives.
- **References from Volunteer Work**: Obtain references from volunteer coordinators or project leads who can vouch for your skills and dedication.

Addressing Employer Concerns

Understanding and addressing employer concerns is key to overcoming the stigma of employment gaps. Here are some common concerns and how to address them:

1. Skill Atrophy

- **Showcase Ongoing Learning**: Highlight any courses, certifications, or training you completed during the gap to demonstrate your commitment to staying current in your field.
- **Demonstrate Practical Experience**: Mention any freelance, consulting, or volunteer work that allowed you to apply and develop your skills.

2. Commitment and Reliability

- **Provide Strong References**: Offer references from individuals who can vouch for your reliability and work ethic during your employment gap.
- **Highlight Relevant Experience**: Focus on experiences that demonstrate your commitment and ability to deliver results, whether through volunteer work, freelance projects, or personal projects.

3. Performance Issues

- **Address Concerns Directly**: If the employment gap was due to performance-related issues, acknowledge any mistakes, and emphasize what you have learned and how you have improved since then.

- **Show Growth and Improvement**: Highlight any steps you have taken to address performance issues, such as additional training, mentorship, or new strategies.

4. **Adaptability**
   - **Highlight Adaptability Skills**: Emphasize your ability to adapt to new environments and technologies, showcasing any experiences that demonstrate this skill.
   - **Showcase Quick Learning**: Mention any situations where you had to quickly learn and adapt to new challenges, whether in a professional, freelance, or volunteer context.

Real-Life Example

Consider the case of Alex, a software developer who took a one-year career break to travel and pursue personal interests. During this time, Alex:

- Volunteered as a technology advisor for a non-profit organization, helping them develop their website and improve their digital presence.
- Completed several online courses in new programming languages and software development techniques.
- Engaged in freelance work, developing websites and applications for small businesses.

When Alex decided to return to the workforce, he addressed his employment gap directly in his resume and cover letter. In his resume, he included a brief mention of his career break and highlighted his volunteer and freelance work. In his cover letter, he explained his career break and emphasized the skills and experiences he gained during this period. During interviews, Alex confidently discussed his gap and provided strong references from his volunteer and freelance work. As a result, he successfully secured a position as a senior software developer at a leading tech company.

The Role of Confidence in Addressing Employment Gaps

Confidence plays a crucial role in overcoming the stigma associated with employment gaps. It is essential to present yourself positively and assertively, both in writing and in person.

Here are some tips to build and project confidence:

1. Practice Your Narrative
- **Rehearse Your Story**: Practice explaining your employment gap in a positive and concise manner. Focus on the skills and experiences you gained during the gap and how they make you a stronger candidate.
- **Stay Positive**: Use positive language and avoid apologizing for the gap. Instead, emphasize the proactive steps you took during the period.

2. Prepare for Common Questions
- **Anticipate Questions**: Be prepared for common questions about employment gaps during

interviews. Practice your responses to these questions to ensure you can answer confidently and succinctly.
- **Highlight Strengths**: Use your responses as an opportunity to highlight your strengths and the value you bring to the role.

3. Use Body Language
- **Maintain Eye Contact**: Make eye contact with the interviewer to convey confidence and engagement.
- **Posture**: Sit or stand up straight and maintain good posture to project confidence.
- **Gestures**: Use hand gestures to emphasize key points and show enthusiasm.

4. **Focus on the Future**
   - **Future Goals**: Emphasize your future goals and how the position aligns with your career aspirations.
   - **Continuous Improvement**: Highlight your commitment to continuous learning and self-improvement.

Changing the Hiring Conversation

As the job market evolves, candidates have more opportunities to influence the hiring conversation. By proactively addressing employment gaps and showcasing their strengths, job seekers can shift the focus from their gaps to their potential. Here are some strategies to change the hiring conversation:

1. **Emphasize Skills and Achievements**
   - **Skills-Based Resumes**: Use a skills-based resume format to highlight your key competencies and achievements rather than focusing on the chronological order of your employment history.
   - **Project-Based Portfolios**: Create a portfolio of projects that demonstrate your skills and achievements, including freelance, volunteer, and personal projects.

2. **Leverage Professional Branding**
   - **Personal Brand**: Develop a strong personal brand that showcases your expertise and unique value proposition. This can include a professional website, a well-crafted

LinkedIn profile, and a consistent online presence.

- **Thought Leadership**: Share your insights and expertise through blog posts, articles, or social media posts. Establishing yourself as a thought leader can help build credibility and shift the focus from your employment gaps to your knowledge and skills.

3. Network Strategically

- **Informational Interviews**: Conduct informational interviews with industry professionals to learn more about potential opportunities and gain insights into the job market. These conversations can also help you build valuable connections.

- **Professional Organizations**: Join professional organizations and attend industry events to expand your network and demonstrate your commitment to your field.

Real-Life Success Stories

To further illustrate the potential for overcoming employment gaps, let's look at some real-life success stories:

1. Emma's Journey Back to the Workforce Emma, a graphic designer, took a two-year career break to care for her young children. During this time, she:
- Volunteered as a graphic designer for a local non-profit organization, creating promotional materials and managing their social media presence.

- Completed several online courses in advanced graphic design and digital marketing.
- Engaged in freelance work, designing logos and marketing materials for small businesses.

When Emma decided to return to the workforce, she addressed her employment gap directly in her resume and cover letter. She highlighted her volunteer and freelance work, emphasizing the skills and experiences she gained during this period. In interviews, Emma confidently discussed her gap and provided strong references from her volunteer and freelance clients. As a result, she successfully secured a full-time position as a senior graphic designer at a marketing agency.

2. John's Career Pivot John, a software engineer, took a one-year break from his career to pursue further education and explore a new field. During this time, he:

- Enrolled in a full-time data science program and earned a certification in data analytics.
- Worked on several data science projects, including analyzing datasets for local businesses and creating predictive models.
- Networked with professionals in the data science field through conferences and online communities.

When John decided to re-enter the workforce, he addressed his employment gap directly in his resume and cover letter. He highlighted his education and data science projects, emphasizing the skills and experiences he gained during this period. In interviews, John confidently discussed his gap and provided references from his data science instructors and project collaborators. As a result, he successfully secured a position as a data analyst at a tech company.

Conclusion

Overcoming the stigma of employment gaps requires a combination of confidence, proactive strategies, and a positive mindset. By reframing the narrative, highlighting relevant activities, and addressing employer concerns directly, job seekers can turn employment gaps into strengths. As the job market continues to evolve, employers are increasingly recognizing the value of diverse career paths and the unique perspectives that come with them. With the right approach, you can confidently navigate the job market and achieve your career goals.

Chapter 3
Strategies for Re-Entering the Workforce

Re-entering the workforce after an employment gap can feel like a daunting task, but with the right strategies, it is entirely achievable. This chapter will explore effective methods for getting back into the job market, including networking, leveraging social media, volunteering, freelancing, and part-time work. By employing these strategies, you can rebuild your career, demonstrate your value to potential employers, and find the job of your dreams.

Section 1: Networking Your Way to Success

1. Building Connections

Networking is one of the most powerful tools for job seekers. It can help you discover hidden job opportunities, gain valuable insights into industries, and receive support from peers and mentors. Here's how to effectively build and expand your professional network:

- **Reconnecting with Old Contacts**: Start by reaching out to former colleagues, supervisors, and clients. Inform them of your job search and ask if they know of any opportunities. Rekindling old relationships can lead to valuable referrals and recommendations.

- **Joining Professional Organizations**: Become a member of industry-specific professional organizations and attend their events. These groups offer networking opportunities, workshops, and seminars that can help you stay informed about industry trends and connect with potential employers.
- **Attending Networking Events**: Participate in networking events, both in-person and virtual. These events are designed to help professionals connect, share knowledge, and explore job opportunities. Be proactive in introducing yourself and discussing your career goals with other attendees.

2. Leveraging Social Media

Social media platforms, particularly LinkedIn, have become essential tools for job seekers. By optimizing your online presence, you can attract recruiters, showcase your expertise, and connect with industry professionals.

- **Optimizing Your LinkedIn Profile**: Ensure your LinkedIn profile is complete, up-to-date, and professional. Use a high-quality profile picture, write a compelling headline, and create a detailed summary that highlights your skills, experiences, and career goals. Include relevant keywords to increase your visibility in search results.
- **Engaging on Professional Platforms**: Actively participate in LinkedIn by sharing articles,

commenting on posts, and joining industry-specific groups. Engage in meaningful conversations and demonstrate your knowledge and expertise. This will help you build your professional brand and connect with potential employers.

- **Showcasing Your Work**: Use LinkedIn's features to showcase your work, such as uploading samples, sharing project updates, and highlighting achievements. This provides tangible evidence of your skills and accomplishments to potential employers.

Section 2: The Power of Volunteering

Volunteering is a highly effective strategy for re-entering the workforce. It not only fills employment gaps but also demonstrates your commitment, helps you gain new skills, and provides valuable references.

1. Volunteering as a Strategy
- **Demonstrating Commitment**: Volunteering shows potential employers that you have remained active and engaged during your employment gap. It demonstrates your dedication to your field and your willingness to contribute.
- **Gaining New Skills**: Volunteering offers opportunities to develop new skills and enhance existing ones. You can take on roles that challenge you and expand your expertise.
- **Building a Network**: Volunteering allows you to meet new people and expand your professional network. You can connect with other volunteers, staff members, and

beneficiaries who may provide job leads or references.

2. Finding Volunteer Opportunities

- **Local Organizations**: Reach out to local non-profits, community centers, and charities to inquire about volunteer opportunities. Many organizations are always in need of help and can offer meaningful roles.
- **Online Platforms**: Use online platforms like VolunteerMatch, Idealist, and LinkedIn to find volunteer opportunities that align with your skills and interests. These platforms allow you to search for roles based on location, cause, and commitment level.
- **Pro Bono Work**: Offer your skills pro bono to organizations or

individuals in need. For example, if you are a graphic designer, you can offer to create marketing materials for a non-profit. Pro bono work can be as valuable as traditional volunteer roles.

3. Showcasing Volunteer Work on Your Resume

- **Include Volunteer Experience**: Create a dedicated section on your resume for volunteer work. List the organizations you volunteered with, your roles, and the impact of your contributions.
- **Highlight Transferable Skills**: Emphasize the skills you gained through volunteering that are relevant to the job you are applying for. This can include project

management, leadership, communication, and technical skills.
- **Using Volunteer References**: Ask for references from volunteer coordinators or project leads. These references can vouch for your abilities, work ethic, and character.

Section 3: Freelance and Part-Time Work

Freelancing and part-time work are excellent ways to bridge employment gaps, maintain your skills, and potentially transition into full-time opportunities.

1. Exploring Freelance Opportunities

- **Platforms for Freelancers**: Use platforms like Upwork, Fiverr, and Freelancer to find freelance opportunities that match your skills. These platforms connect freelancers with clients seeking various services, from writing and graphic design to programming and marketing.

- **Building a Portfolio**: Create a portfolio of your freelance work to showcase your expertise and accomplishments. Include samples of your work, client testimonials, and a list of projects you have completed.
- **Setting Competitive Rates**: Research industry standards and set competitive rates for your services. Consider your experience, skill level, and the complexity of the projects when determining your rates.

2. **Finding Part-Time Work**
   - **Job Boards and Company Websites**: Use job boards like

Indeed, Glassdoor, and LinkedIn to search for part-time opportunities. Check company websites for part-time job listings and apply directly.

- **Staffing Agencies**: Register with staffing agencies that specialize in part-time and temporary placements. These agencies can match you with suitable roles and provide support throughout the application process.
- **Networking**: Leverage your professional network to find part-time opportunities. Inform your contacts that you are seeking part-time work and ask for referrals or recommendations.

3. **Building a Portfolio**
    - **Showcasing Freelance and Part-Time Work**: Create a

comprehensive portfolio that includes samples of your freelance and part-time work. Highlight projects that demonstrate your skills, creativity, and problem-solving abilities.

- **Emphasizing Achievements**: Focus on the results and impact of your work. Use metrics and specific examples to showcase your accomplishments, such as increased sales, improved efficiency, or successful project completions.

Conclusion

Re-entering the workforce after an employment gap requires a strategic approach that leverages networking, social media, volunteering, and freelancing opportunities. By building connections, optimizing your online presence, engaging in meaningful volunteer work, and exploring freelance and part-time roles, you can demonstrate your value to potential employers and achieve your career goals. With dedication and persistence, you can successfully navigate the job market and find the job of your dreams.

Chapter 4
Crafting Your Winning Resume

Your resume is often the first impression you make on potential employers. It should effectively showcase your skills, experiences, and accomplishments while minimizing the impact of any employment gaps. This chapter will provide you with strategies to create a compelling resume that highlights your strengths and positions you as a strong candidate for your desired job.

Highlighting Your Strengths

When crafting your resume, focus on showcasing your skills, achievements, and experiences that demonstrate your value to potential employers. Here are some key tips to help you highlight your strengths:

1. **Professional Summary**
   - **Concise and Compelling**: Start your resume with a professional summary that provides a brief overview of your qualifications, experiences, and career goals. Keep it concise and focused on your most relevant achievements.
   - **Tailored to the Job**: Customize your professional summary for each job application, emphasizing the skills and experiences that align with the job description.

Example:

Dynamic and results-oriented marketing professional with over five years of experience in developing and executing successful marketing campaigns. Proven track record of increasing brand awareness and driving sales through strategic planning and innovative marketing techniques. Seeking a challenging role in a fast-paced environment where I can leverage my skills to contribute to the company's growth.

2. Key Skills

- **Relevant Skills**: List your key skills that are relevant to the job you are applying for. Focus on both hard and soft skills that demonstrate your ability to excel in the role.

- **Quantifiable Achievements**: Whenever possible, quantify your skills with specific achievements. For example, "Increased sales by 30%" or "Managed a team of 10 employees."

Example:

Key Skills:
- Project Management: Successfully managed multiple projects from inception to completion, ensuring timely delivery and adherence to budgets.
- Digital Marketing: Expertise in developing and executing digital marketing strategies, resulting in a 25% increase in online engagement.
- Communication: Strong verbal and written communication skills, with a

proven ability to build relationships with clients and stakeholders.

- Data Analysis: Proficient in analyzing data to identify trends and make data-driven decisions.

- Leadership: Demonstrated leadership abilities, with experience in managing and mentoring teams.

3. Professional Experience

- **Reverse Chronological Order**: List your work experience in reverse chronological order, starting with your most recent job. For each position, include your job title, company name, location, and dates of employment.
- **Accomplishments Over Duties**: Focus on your accomplishments and contributions rather than just listing your job duties. Use action verbs

and quantify your achievements to make them more impactful.

Example:

Professional Experience:
Marketing Manager
XYZ Company, New York, NY
January 2018 – Present

- Developed and executed comprehensive marketing strategies that increased brand awareness by 40%.
- Managed a team of 10 marketing professionals, providing mentorship and guidance to achieve departmental goals.
- Coordinated cross-functional teams to deliver successful product launches, resulting in a 20% increase in sales.
- Analyzed market trends and consumer behavior to inform marketing decisions and optimize campaign performance.

Marketing Specialist
ABC Corporation, New York, NY
June 2015 – December 2017

- Designed and implemented marketing campaigns that boosted customer engagement by 30%.
- Collaborated with the sales team to develop targeted marketing materials, contributing to a 15% increase in lead generation.
- Conducted market research to identify new opportunities and inform marketing strategies.
- Managed social media accounts, growing the company's online presence and follower base.

Creative Formatting

Using creative formatting can help de-emphasize employment gaps and draw attention to your skills and accomplishments. Here are some formatting tips to consider:

1. Functional Resume

A functional resume focuses on your skills and accomplishments rather than your chronological work history. This format can be particularly useful for individuals with significant employment gaps or career changers.

Example:

Jane Doe
jane.doe@example.com | LinkedIn: [linkedin.com/in/janedoe](https://www.linkedin.com/in/janedoe) | +123-456-7890

Professional Summary:
Dynamic and results-oriented professional with a proven track record in marketing and project management. Adept at developing and executing successful marketing campaigns, leading teams, and driving business growth.

Key Skills:
- Project Management
- Digital Marketing
- Communication
- Data Analysis
- Leadership

Professional Experience:
Marketing Manager
XYZ Company, New York, NY
January 2018 – Present

Marketing Specialist
ABC Corporation, New York, NY
June 2015 – December 2017

Education and Certifications:
- Bachelor of Science in Marketing, University of New York
- Digital Marketing Certification, Google
- Project Management Professional (PMP) Certification

2. Hybrid Resume

A hybrid resume combines elements of both chronological and functional resumes. It allows you to highlight your skills and accomplishments while also providing a chronological work history.

Example:

Jane Doe
jane.doe@example.com | LinkedIn: [linkedin.com/in/janedoe](https://www.linkedin.com/in/janedoe) | +123-456-7890

Professional Summary:
Dynamic and results-oriented professional with over five years of experience in marketing and project management. Proven track record of developing and executing successful marketing campaigns, leading teams, and driving business growth.

Key Skills:

- Project Management
- Digital Marketing
- Communication
- Data Analysis
- Leadership

Professional Experience:

Marketing Manager

XYZ Company, New York, NY

January 2018 – Present

- Developed and executed comprehensive marketing strategies that increased brand awareness by 40%.
- Managed a team of 10 marketing professionals, providing mentorship and guidance to achieve departmental goals.

Marketing Specialist

ABC Corporation, New York, NY

June 2015 – December 2017

- Designed and implemented marketing campaigns that boosted customer engagement by 30%.
- Collaborated with the sales team to develop targeted marketing materials, contributing to a 15% increase in lead generation.

Education and Certifications:
- Bachelor of Science in Marketing, University of New York
- Digital Marketing Certification, Google
- Project Management Professional (PMP) Certification

Positive Spin on Employment Gaps

Turning employment gaps into positives can help mitigate any concerns potential employers may have. Here are some strategies to achieve this:

1. Highlighting Relevant Activities

- **Volunteer Work**: Mention any volunteer work, pro bono projects, or community involvement. These activities demonstrate commitment and a proactive approach.
- **Freelancing and Consulting**: If you took on freelance or consulting work during the gap, highlight these experiences and the skills you developed.
- **Education and Skill Development**: Emphasize any courses, certifications, or training you completed during the gap.

Example:

Volunteer Experience:
Project Coordinator
Non-Profit Organization, New York, NY
April 2020 – Present

- Managed a team of volunteers for various community projects.
- Developed project plans and coordinated resources to ensure successful project completion.

Freelance Consultant
April 2020 – Present

- Provided strategic advice and marketing services to small businesses.
- Developed customized marketing strategies to enhance brand visibility.

2. Reframing the Narrative

- **Positive Framing**: Present the gap as a time of personal and professional development. Highlight the new skills, experiences, and perspectives you gained during this period.

- **Focus on Achievements**: Emphasize any accomplishments during the gap, such as certifications earned, courses completed, or volunteer projects led.

Example:

Career Break for Skill Development
June 2019 – March 2020

- Completed a digital marketing certification course to enhance my skills and stay current with industry trends.
- Volunteered as a marketing coordinator for a local non-profit organization, managing social media campaigns and increasing community engagement.

Conclusion

Crafting a winning resume involves strategically highlighting your strengths, using creative formatting to minimize employment gaps, and turning those gaps into positive experiences. By focusing on your skills, accomplishments, and relevant activities, you can create a compelling resume that positions you as a strong candidate for your desired job. With the right approach, your resume will stand out to potential employers and open doors to new opportunities.

Chapter 5
Acing the Interview

The interview is a critical step in the job search process. It's your opportunity to showcase your skills, experiences, and personality, and to convince the employer that you are the best fit for the role. This chapter will explore strategies to prepare for interviews, address employment gaps confidently, and leave a lasting impression on potential employers.

Preparation is Key

Effective preparation is essential to acing any interview. Here are some key steps to take before your interview:

1. Research the Company

- **Understand the Company's Mission and Values**: Familiarize yourself with the company's mission, values, and culture. This will help you align your responses with what the company is looking for in a candidate.
- **Know the Industry**: Stay informed about the industry trends and challenges that the company is facing. This shows that you are knowledgeable and genuinely interested in the field.
- **Review the Job Description**: Carefully read the job description and identify the key skills and qualifications required for the role. Think about how your experiences and skills match these requirements.

2. Practice Common Interview Questions

While every interview is unique, there are common questions that you can anticipate. Practicing these questions will help you articulate your responses clearly and confidently.

- **Tell Me About Yourself**: Prepare a concise and compelling summary of your professional background, highlighting your key achievements and how they relate to the role.
- **Why Do You Want to Work Here?**: Craft a response that shows your enthusiasm for the company and how your values align with theirs.
- **What Are Your Strengths and Weaknesses?**: Focus on strengths that are relevant to the job and

provide examples of how you have demonstrated these strengths. For weaknesses, mention a genuine area for improvement and the steps you are taking to address it.

- **Describe a Challenge You've Faced and How You Overcame It**: Use the STAR method (Situation, Task, Action, Result) to structure your response and highlight your problem-solving skills.

3. Prepare Questions for the Interviewer

Asking thoughtful questions shows that you are engaged and interested in the role. Here are some questions to consider:

- **Can you tell me more about the team I would be working with?**

- **What are the key challenges the company is currently facing?**
- **How do you measure success in this role?**
- **What opportunities are there for professional development and growth?**

Addressing the Gap

Addressing employment gaps confidently and positively is crucial during interviews. Here are some strategies to help you discuss your employment gap:

1. Be Honest and Concise

- **Provide a Brief Explanation**: Offer a concise and honest explanation for your employment gap. For example, "I took a career break to care for a family member," or "I pursued further education to enhance my skills."

- **Focus on the Positive**: Emphasize the positive aspects of your employment gap, such as new skills acquired, volunteer work, or freelance projects.

2. Highlight Relevant Experiences

- **Discuss What You Learned**: Talk about the skills and experiences you gained during the gap and how they make you a better candidate for the role. For example, "During my career break, I completed a certification in project management, which has equipped me with new strategies to manage projects effectively."
- **Mention Ongoing Engagement**: If you stayed engaged with your

industry through freelance work, volunteering, or continued education, highlight these activities. For example, "During my employment gap, I volunteered as a marketing coordinator for a local non-profit, which allowed me to develop my digital marketing skills."

3. **Practice Your Response**
   - **Rehearse with a Friend**: Practice discussing your employment gap with a friend or mentor to gain confidence. They can provide feedback and help you refine your response.
   - **Stay Positive and Confident**: Maintain a positive and confident tone when discussing your employment gap. Avoid apologizing or sounding defensive. Instead,

focus on how the gap has contributed to your personal and professional growth.

Making a Strong Impression

Making a strong impression during an interview involves more than just answering questions. Here are some tips to leave a lasting positive impression on your interviewers:

1. Dress Appropriately
- **Professional Attire**: Choose attire that is appropriate for the company's culture and the role you are applying for. When in doubt, it's better to be slightly overdressed than underdressed.
- **Grooming**: Ensure that you are well-groomed and presentable. Pay

attention to details such as clean nails, polished shoes, and neat hair.

2. Show Enthusiasm and Positivity

- **Positive Body Language**: Use positive body language, such as maintaining eye contact, smiling, and nodding. These non-verbal cues convey confidence and engagement.
- **Genuine Enthusiasm**: Show genuine enthusiasm for the role and the company. Express your excitement about the opportunity and how you can contribute to the organization's success.

3. Build Rapport with the Interviewer

- **Find Common Ground**: Look for opportunities to find common ground with the interviewer. This could be shared interests, experiences, or values. Building rapport can help create a positive and memorable interaction.

- **Active Listening**: Practice active listening by paying close attention to the interviewer's questions and responses. Show that you are engaged by nodding, making eye contact, and providing thoughtful answers.

4. **Follow-Up After the Interview**
    - **Send a Thank-You Email**: Send a thank-you email within 24 hours of the interview. Express your appreciation for the opportunity to interview and reiterate your interest in the role. Mention specific points from the interview that resonated

with you and highlight why you are a strong fit for the position.
- **Stay Professional**: Keep your thank-you email professional and concise. Avoid overly casual language or making demands.

Example Thank-You Email:

Subject: Thank You - [Your Name]

Dear [Interviewer's Name],

Thank you for the opportunity to interview for the [Job Title] position at [Company Name]. I appreciate the time you took to discuss the role and learn more about my background.

I am very excited about the possibility of joining [Company Name] and contributing to [specific aspect of the company or role discussed in the interview]. I believe my skills and experiences, particularly in [specific skills or experiences], would be a valuable asset to your team.

Thank you once again for your consideration. I look forward to the possibility of working with you and contributing to the success of [Company Name].

Best regards,
[Your Name]
[Your Phone Number]
[Your Email Address]

Overcoming Anxiety and Building Confidence

Interview anxiety is common, but there are strategies to manage it and build confidence:

1. Prepare Thoroughly

- **Mock Interviews**: Conduct mock interviews with a friend, mentor, or career coach. This practice can help you become more comfortable with the interview format and questions.
- **Research**: The more you know about the company and the role, the more confident you will feel. Preparation helps reduce uncertainty and boost confidence.

2. Practice Relaxation Techniques

- **Deep Breathing**: Practice deep breathing exercises to calm your nerves before the interview. Inhale deeply through your nose, hold for a few seconds, and exhale slowly through your mouth.
- **Positive Visualization**: Visualize yourself succeeding in the interview. Imagine walking into the

room with confidence, answering questions effectively, and leaving a positive impression.

3. Focus on the Present
- **Stay Present**: Focus on the present moment rather than worrying about the outcome. Concentrate on the interviewer's questions and your responses, rather than overthinking the overall interview.
- **Take It One Step at a Time**: Break the interview into manageable steps. Focus on each question individually rather than worrying about the entire process.

4. Build Self-Confidence
- **Self-Affirmations**: Use positive self-affirmations to boost your

confidence. Remind yourself of your strengths and accomplishments.

- **Reflect on Successes**: Reflect on past successes and positive experiences. Remind yourself of times when you overcame challenges and achieved your goals.

Conclusion

Acing the interview is a combination of thorough preparation, confident communication, and a positive mindset. By researching the company, practicing common interview questions, addressing employment gaps confidently, and making a strong impression, you can increase your chances of securing the job. Remember to stay calm, be yourself, and demonstrate your enthusiasm for the role. With the right approach, you can successfully navigate the interview process and move one step closer to achieving your career goals.

Chapter 6
Mindset and Mental Health

Finding work after a long period of unemployment can be a challenging and emotionally taxing journey. Addressing the mental health aspects of unemployment and building a resilient mindset are crucial for success. This chapter will explore practical advice for managing anxiety, depression, and low self-esteem, and provide strategies to boost confidence and maintain a positive outlook throughout the job search process.

Dealing with Anxiety and Depression

Unemployment can lead to feelings of anxiety and depression, which can impact your motivation and overall well-being. Here are some practical tips to manage these challenges:

1. Recognize and Acknowledge Your Feelings

- **Self-Awareness**: Pay attention to your emotions and acknowledge that feeling anxious or depressed during unemployment is normal. Recognizing your feelings is the first step toward addressing them.
- **Journaling**: Keep a journal to document your thoughts and emotions. Writing can help you process your feelings and gain clarity on your experiences.

2. **Seek Professional Help**
    - **Therapy and Counseling**: Consider seeking support from a therapist or counselor. Professional guidance can help you develop coping strategies and address any underlying issues contributing to your anxiety or depression.
    - **Support Groups**: Join support groups or online communities where you can connect with others who are going through similar experiences. Sharing your struggles and hearing from others can provide comfort and encouragement.

3. **Practice Self-Care**
    - **Physical Health**: Take care of your physical health by maintaining a balanced diet, exercising regularly, and getting enough sleep. Physical

well-being is closely linked to mental health.

- **Relaxation Techniques**: Incorporate relaxation techniques such as deep breathing, meditation, and mindfulness into your daily routine. These practices can help reduce stress and improve your overall sense of well-being.
- **Hobbies and Interests**: Engage in activities that bring you joy and fulfillment. Pursuing hobbies and interests can provide a sense of purpose and help distract you from negative thoughts.

Building Confidence

Building confidence is essential for a successful job search. Here are some strategies to boost your self-esteem and present yourself confidently to potential employers:

1. Focus on Your Strengths

- **Identify Your Strengths**: Make a list of your skills, accomplishments, and positive qualities. Remind yourself of what you have achieved and what makes you valuable as a candidate.
- **Leverage Your Strengths**: Highlight your strengths in your resume, cover letter, and during interviews. Focus on how your skills and experiences can contribute to the success of the company.

2. Set Realistic Goals

- **Short-Term and Long-Term Goals**: Set both short-term and long-term goals for your job search.

Break these goals into manageable steps and celebrate your progress along the way.

- **Achievable Milestones**: Set achievable milestones, such as applying for a certain number of jobs each week or attending networking events. Achieving these milestones can boost your confidence and keep you motivated.

3. Positive Self-Talk

- **Affirmations**: Use positive affirmations to boost your self-esteem. Remind yourself of your worth and potential with statements like, "I am capable and deserving of success," or "I have valuable skills to offer."
- **Counter Negative Thoughts**: Challenge negative thoughts and

replace them with positive and constructive ones. Instead of thinking, "I'll never find a job," reframe it as, "I am taking proactive steps to find the right opportunity."

4. Practice Interview Skills

- **Mock Interviews**: Conduct mock interviews with a friend, mentor, or career coach. Practice answering common interview questions and receive feedback to improve your responses.
- **Confidence Building Exercises**: Practice exercises that boost your confidence, such as power posing or visualization techniques. These exercises can help you feel more self-assured during interviews.

Maintaining a Positive Outlook

Maintaining a positive outlook is vital for navigating the ups and downs of the job search process. Here are some tips to help you stay optimistic:

1. Stay Connected with a Support System

- **Family and Friends**: Lean on your family and friends for support and encouragement. Share your job search experiences with them and seek their advice and guidance.
- **Networking Connections**: Stay connected with your professional network. Reach out to former colleagues, mentors, and industry contacts for support and potential job leads.

2. Focus on Continuous Improvement

- **Learn New Skills**: Use your time to learn new skills or enhance existing ones. Enroll in online courses, attend workshops, or pursue certifications that are relevant to your career goals.
- **Stay Informed**: Keep up-to-date with industry trends and developments. This shows potential employers that you are proactive and committed to staying current in your field.

3. Celebrate Small Wins

- **Acknowledge Achievements**: Celebrate small wins and milestones in your job search. Whether it's completing a new course, updating your resume, or securing an interview, acknowledge your achievements and take pride in your progress.

- **Stay Motivated**: Use your accomplishments to stay motivated. Remind yourself that each step brings you closer to your ultimate goal.

4. Practice Gratitude

- **Daily Gratitude**: Practice gratitude by reflecting on the positive aspects of your life each day. Write down three things you are grateful for, no matter how small. This practice can shift your focus from what's missing to what you have.
- **Gratitude Journal**: Keep a gratitude journal where you document moments of gratitude and positivity. Reviewing this journal can boost your mood and

remind you of the good things in your life.

Real-Life Example

Consider the story of David, a graphic designer who faced a challenging period of unemployment after being laid off. David struggled with feelings of anxiety and low self-esteem, but he took proactive steps to manage his mental health and build his confidence.

- **Therapy and Support Groups**: David sought professional help and joined support groups to address his anxiety and depression. This support system provided him with coping strategies and a sense of community.

- **Skill Development**: During his unemployment, David enrolled in online courses to learn new graphic design techniques and software. This not only enhanced his skills but also gave him a sense of accomplishment.
- **Networking**: David reconnected with former colleagues and attended industry events to expand his professional network. These connections provided valuable job leads and support.
- **Positive Mindset**: David practiced positive self-talk and used affirmations to boost his confidence. He focused on his strengths and set realistic goals for his job search.

With these strategies, David was able to overcome his anxiety and regain his confidence. He eventually secured a new position as a senior graphic designer, where he could apply his enhanced skills and continue to grow professionally.

Conclusion

Managing your mental health and building a positive mindset are crucial components of a successful job search. By addressing anxiety and depression, focusing on your strengths, setting realistic goals, and maintaining a positive outlook, you can navigate the challenges of re-entering the workforce with confidence. Remember that seeking support and practicing self-care are essential steps in this journey. With determination and resilience, you can overcome obstacles and achieve your career goals.

Chapter 7
Daily Routines for Success

Establishing effective daily routines is essential for productivity, well-being, and success in your job search. Having a structured routine can help you stay organized, motivated, and focused. This chapter will explore the importance of daily routines, provide practical tips for creating a productive schedule, and highlight the benefits of maintaining a healthy lifestyle.

Creating Structure

A well-structured daily routine can provide a sense of purpose and direction, especially during periods of unemployment. Here are some key steps to create a productive daily schedule:

1. Start with a Morning Routine

- **Consistent Wake-Up Time**: Set a consistent wake-up time each day to establish a regular sleep pattern. This can help regulate your body clock and improve your overall energy levels.
- **Morning Rituals**: Incorporate morning rituals that set a positive tone for the day. This could include activities such as meditation, journaling, exercise, or reading. Morning rituals can help you feel grounded and focused.

Example Morning Routine:

7:00 AM: Wake up and stretch

7:15 AM: Meditation and deep breathing exercises

7:30 AM: Healthy breakfast

8:00 AM: Review daily goals and to-do list

8:15 AM: Physical exercise (e.g., a walk, yoga, or workout)

2. Plan Your Day

- **Set Daily Goals**: Write down your daily goals and prioritize tasks that are most important. Breaking your goals into manageable tasks can make them more achievable and less overwhelming.
- **Time Blocking**: Use time blocking to allocate specific periods for different activities. This helps ensure that you dedicate time to

important tasks and avoid distractions.

Example Daily Schedule:

8:30 AM - 10:30 AM: Job search and applications

10:30 AM - 11:00 AM: Break and light snack

11:00 AM - 12:30 PM: Networking and reaching out to contacts

12:30 PM - 1:30 PM: Lunch and relaxation

1:30 PM - 3:00 PM: Skill development (e.g., online courses or certifications)

3:00 PM - 3:30 PM: Break and physical activity (e.g., a walk or stretching)

3:30 PM - 5:00 PM: Resume writing and cover letters

5:00 PM - 6:00 PM: Personal projects or hobbies

3. Review and Reflect
- **End-of-Day Reflection**: Take time at the end of each day to review your accomplishments and reflect on what went well. Identify areas for improvement and set intentions for the next day.
- **Gratitude Practice**: Incorporate a gratitude practice to end your day on a positive note. Reflect on things you are grateful for and acknowledge the progress you have made.

Healthy Lifestyle

Maintaining a healthy lifestyle is crucial for both physical and mental well-being. Here are some tips for incorporating healthy habits into your daily routine:

1. **Prioritize Physical Health**
   - **Regular Exercise**: Aim for at least 30 minutes of physical activity each day. Exercise can boost your mood, improve energy levels, and reduce stress.
   - **Balanced Diet**: Eat a balanced diet that includes a variety of fruits, vegetables, whole grains, lean proteins, and healthy fats. Proper nutrition supports overall health and cognitive function.
   - **Stay Hydrated**: Drink plenty of water throughout the day to stay hydrated. Dehydration can lead to fatigue and decreased concentration.

2. **Focus on Mental Health**
   - **Mindfulness and Meditation**: Practice mindfulness and meditation

to reduce stress and improve mental clarity. Even a few minutes of mindfulness each day can have a positive impact.

- **Social Connections**: Stay connected with friends and family. Social interactions can provide support, reduce feelings of isolation, and enhance your well-being.
- **Limit Screen Time**: Be mindful of your screen time, especially on social media. Excessive screen time can lead to increased stress and anxiety.

3. Prioritize Sleep

- **Consistent Sleep Schedule**: Establish a consistent sleep schedule by going to bed and waking up at the same time each

day. Aim for 7-9 hours of quality sleep each night.
- **Relaxing Bedtime Routine**: Create a relaxing bedtime routine to wind down before sleep. This could include activities such as reading, listening to calming music, or taking a warm bath.

Productivity Tips

Boosting productivity involves finding strategies that work best for you. Here are some additional tips to enhance your productivity:

1. Use Productivity Tools
- **Task Management Apps**: Use task management apps like Trello, Todoist, or Asana to organize your tasks and track your progress.

These tools can help you stay on top of your responsibilities and deadlines.

- **Calendar Scheduling**: Utilize calendar apps to schedule your tasks and appointments. Blocking out time for specific activities ensures that you allocate enough time for each task.

2. Minimize Distractions

- **Create a Dedicated Workspace**: Set up a dedicated workspace that is free from distractions. Having a designated area for work can help you stay focused and productive.
- **Limit Interruptions**: Minimize interruptions by setting boundaries with family or housemates. Inform them of your work schedule and ask

for their cooperation in respecting your focused time.

3. Take Breaks

- **Pomodoro Technique**: Use the Pomodoro Technique to break your work into intervals, typically 25 minutes of focused work followed by a 5-minute break. This method can enhance productivity and prevent burnout.
- **Short Breaks**: Take short breaks throughout the day to rest and recharge. Use these breaks to stretch, take a walk, or engage in a brief relaxation activity.

Real-Life Example

Consider the story of Lisa, a marketing professional who faced a challenging job search after being laid off. Lisa realized the importance of establishing a structured daily routine and maintaining a healthy lifestyle to stay productive and positive.

- **Morning Routine**: Lisa started her day with meditation, a healthy breakfast, and a brisk walk. This routine helped her feel energized and focused.
- **Daily Planning**: Each morning, Lisa set specific goals for her job search, networking, and skill development. She used a task management app to organize her tasks and track her progress.
- **Healthy Habits**: Lisa prioritized her physical health by incorporating regular exercise and balanced meals into her routine. She also

practiced mindfulness and limited her screen time to reduce stress.
- **End-of-Day Reflection**: At the end of each day, Lisa reviewed her accomplishments and reflected on what she was grateful for. This practice helped her stay motivated and maintain a positive outlook.

With these strategies, Lisa was able to stay organized, motivated, and healthy throughout her job search. She eventually secured a new position in marketing, where she could apply her skills and continue to grow professionally.

Conclusion

Establishing effective daily routines and maintaining a healthy lifestyle are essential for productivity, well-being, and success in your job search. By creating structure, prioritizing physical and mental health, and using productivity tools, you can stay organized, motivated, and focused. Remember that consistency and self-care are key components of a successful routine. With the right approach, you can navigate the challenges of unemployment and achieve your career goals.

Chapter 8
Continuous Learning and Skill Development

In today's fast-paced job market, continuous learning and skill development are crucial for staying competitive and achieving long-term career success. Embracing a growth mindset and committing to lifelong learning can help you adapt to changing industry trends, enhance your skill set, and open up new opportunities. This chapter will explore the importance of continuous learning, provide resources for skill development, and offer strategies to integrate learning into your daily routine.

The Importance of Continuous Learning

Continuous learning refers to the ongoing process of acquiring new skills, knowledge, and experiences throughout your career. Here are some key reasons why continuous learning is essential:

1. Staying Relevant in Your Field
- **Adapting to Changes**: Industries are constantly evolving, driven by technological advancements, market dynamics, and changing consumer preferences. Continuous learning helps you stay updated with the latest trends and technologies, ensuring that your skills remain relevant.
- **Enhancing Competitiveness**: Employers value candidates who

demonstrate a commitment to self-improvement and continuous learning. Developing new skills can set you apart from other candidates and increase your competitiveness in the job market.

2. Expanding Career Opportunities

- **Career Growth**: Learning new skills can open up opportunities for career advancement and higher-level positions. It enables you to take on new responsibilities and challenges, contributing to your professional growth.
- **Career Transition**: Continuous learning can facilitate career transitions by equipping you with the skills needed to pivot to a new industry or role. It provides the

flexibility to explore different career paths and interests.

3. Personal Fulfillment

- **Intellectual Curiosity**: Engaging in continuous learning satisfies intellectual curiosity and promotes personal growth. It keeps your mind active and encourages a love for learning.
- **Boosting Confidence**: Acquiring new skills and knowledge boosts your confidence and self-esteem. It empowers you to take on new challenges and approach your career with a positive mindset.

Resources for Skill Development

There are numerous resources available to support continuous learning and skill development. Here are some valuable options to consider:

1. Online Courses and Certifications

- **Coursera**: Offers a wide range of courses and certifications from top universities and institutions. Courses cover various subjects, from technology and business to arts and humanities.
- **edX**: Provides online courses and programs from renowned universities and organizations. You can earn verified certificates or pursue micro-degrees in specific fields.
- **LinkedIn Learning**: Offers a vast library of video tutorials and courses on topics such as business, technology, creative skills, and personal development. Courses are

taught by industry experts and provide practical insights.

2. Workshops and Webinars

- **Industry Conferences**: Attend industry conferences and workshops to learn from experts, gain insights into the latest trends, and network with professionals.
- **Professional Associations**: Join professional associations related to your field. Many associations offer workshops, webinars, and training sessions to help members stay updated with industry developments.

3. Books and Publications

- **Books**: Reading books on your field of interest is a great way to gain in-depth knowledge and insights. Look

for recommendations from industry leaders and professionals.
- **Industry Journals**: Subscribe to industry journals and publications to stay informed about the latest research, trends, and best practices in your field.

4. **Mentorship and Coaching**
   - **Mentorship Programs**: Seek out mentorship programs within your organization or industry. A mentor can provide guidance, share experiences, and help you navigate your career path.
   - **Career Coaching**: Consider working with a career coach to identify your strengths, set career goals, and develop a personalized learning plan. A coach can provide

valuable feedback and support your professional development.

Strategies for Integrating Learning into Your Routine

Integrating continuous learning into your daily routine requires commitment and effective time management. Here are some strategies to help you make learning a regular part of your life:

1. Set Clear Learning Goals
- **Identify Areas for Improvement**: Assess your current skills and identify areas where you need improvement or want to gain new knowledge. Set specific, measurable, achievable, relevant, and time-bound (SMART) learning goals.

- **Align with Career Objectives**: Ensure that your learning goals align with your long-term career objectives. Focus on acquiring skills that will help you advance in your current role or transition to a new one.

2. **Create a Learning Schedule**
    - **Allocate Time for Learning**: Dedicate specific time blocks in your daily or weekly schedule for learning activities. Consistency is key, so make learning a non-negotiable part of your routine.
    - **Balance with Other Commitments**: Balance your learning schedule with other commitments, such as work, family, and personal activities. Prioritize

your tasks to ensure that learning remains a priority.

3. Use Microlearning Techniques

- **Short Learning Sessions**: Break down your learning activities into small, manageable sessions. Microlearning allows you to absorb information in bite-sized chunks, making it easier to retain and apply.
- **Leverage Mobile Learning**: Use mobile apps and platforms to access learning materials on the go. This allows you to make use of spare moments, such as during commutes or waiting times.

4. Apply What You Learn

- **Practical Application**: Apply the skills and knowledge you acquire in real-life scenarios. Look for

opportunities to use new skills in your current role, volunteer projects, or personal projects.
- **Continuous Improvement**: Reflect on your learning experiences and seek feedback. Identify areas for improvement and make necessary adjustments to enhance your skills.

Real-Life Example

Consider the story of Rachel, a project manager who faced a period of unemployment due to company downsizing. Rachel decided to use this time to focus on continuous learning and skill development.

- **Online Courses**: Rachel enrolled in online courses on project management, data analysis, and agile methodologies. She earned certifications in these areas, which enhanced her skill set and made her more competitive in the job market.

- **Industry Workshops**: She attended industry workshops and webinars to stay updated with the latest trends and best practices in project management. These events also provided networking opportunities with professionals in her field.
- **Books and Publications**: Rachel read books and industry journals to gain deeper insights into project management and leadership. She applied the knowledge gained from these readings to her volunteer projects.

- **Mentorship**: Rachel joined a mentorship program through a professional association. Her mentor provided guidance, shared valuable experiences, and helped her navigate her career transition.

By integrating continuous learning into her daily routine, Rachel not only enhanced her skills but also regained her confidence and motivation. She eventually secured a new position as a senior project manager, where she could apply her newly acquired skills and continue to grow professionally.

Conclusion

Continuous learning and skill development are essential for staying competitive and achieving long-term career success. By embracing a growth mindset, setting clear learning goals, and integrating learning into your daily routine, you can enhance your skills, expand your career opportunities, and achieve personal fulfillment. Remember that learning is a lifelong journey, and staying committed to self-improvement will help you navigate the ever-evolving job market with confidence and resilience.

Chapter 9
Real-Life Success Stories

Real-life success stories can serve as powerful sources of inspiration and motivation for job seekers who are navigating employment gaps. These stories illustrate the challenges faced by individuals, the strategies they employed to overcome those challenges, and the eventual successes they achieved. This chapter will highlight several real-life success stories of individuals who found meaningful employment after significant periods of unemployment. Each story will provide insights into the practical steps they took, the mindset shifts they experienced, and the support systems that helped them along the way.

Story 1: Sarah's Journey from Unemployment to Entrepreneurship

Background

Sarah, a marketing professional, found herself unemployed after her company underwent a massive restructuring. After nearly a decade in the corporate world, she was suddenly without a job. The uncertainty of her future led to feelings of anxiety and self-doubt. However, Sarah decided to use this period of unemployment as an opportunity for self-reflection and growth.

Strategies Employed

1. **Skill Development**: Sarah enrolled in online courses to

enhance her digital marketing skills. She completed certifications in social media marketing, content creation, and search engine optimization (SEO). This not only kept her skills up-to-date but also boosted her confidence.

2. **Freelancing**: To maintain an income stream and gain practical experience, Sarah started freelancing. She offered her marketing services to small businesses and non-profits. This allowed her to build a diverse portfolio and expand her professional network.

3. **Networking**: Sarah actively participated in industry events and joined marketing groups on LinkedIn. She reached out to former colleagues and attended webinars

to stay connected with the latest industry trends.

4. **Personal Branding**: Sarah created a personal website and blog where she shared her insights on marketing trends and strategies. This showcased her expertise and attracted potential clients and employers.

Outcome

Over time, Sarah's freelance business grew, and she realized that entrepreneurship was a viable path for her. She officially launched her own digital marketing agency, which quickly gained traction due to her strong network and reputation. Today, Sarah's agency serves a diverse clientele, and she has found fulfillment in her entrepreneurial journey.

Story 2: John's Transition from IT to Data Science

Background
John, an IT specialist, faced a layoff after the company he worked for was acquired by a larger corporation. With over 15 years of experience in IT, John was at a crossroads and unsure about his next steps. The job market for traditional IT roles was highly competitive, and John realized that he needed to adapt to the changing landscape.

Strategies Employed
1. **Re-skilling**: John identified data science as a growing field with strong demand. He enrolled in a comprehensive data science bootcamp, where he learned programming languages like

Python, data analysis techniques, and machine learning algorithms.

2. **Project Work**: To gain hands-on experience, John worked on various data science projects. He analyzed datasets, built predictive models, and created data visualizations. He documented these projects in a portfolio to demonstrate his capabilities.

3. **Certifications**: John obtained certifications in data science from reputable institutions, such as Coursera and edX. These certifications added credibility to his resume and showcased his commitment to learning.

4. **Networking and Mentorship**: John joined data science communities, both online and offline. He attended meetups,

participated in hackathons, and sought mentorship from experienced data scientists who provided guidance and feedback.

Outcome

John successfully transitioned into a new career as a data scientist. His portfolio and certifications helped him secure a role at a tech company, where he applies his data science skills to solve complex business problems. John's story demonstrates the importance of adaptability and the value of continuous learning.

Story 3: Emma's Return to the Workforce After Maternity Leave

Background

Emma, a finance professional, took a two-year break from her career to care for her young children. As her maternity leave came to an end, Emma felt both excited and anxious about re-entering the workforce. She was concerned about how employers would perceive her employment gap and whether her skills were still relevant.

Strategies Employed

1. **Stay Updated**: During her maternity leave, Emma made a conscious effort to stay updated with industry developments. She subscribed to financial journals, attended webinars, and participated

in online courses related to finance and accounting.

2. **Volunteering**: Emma volunteered as a treasurer for a local non-profit organization. This allowed her to apply her financial skills in a practical setting and fill her employment gap with meaningful experience.

3. **Professional Networking**: Emma reconnected with former colleagues and joined finance-related networking groups. She attended industry events and reached out to professionals in her field for advice and job leads.

4. **Resume and Interview Preparation**: Emma worked with a career coach to update her resume and practice her interview skills. She learned how to address her

employment gap confidently and emphasize the skills she gained during her maternity leave.

Outcome

Emma successfully re-entered the workforce and secured a role as a financial analyst at a reputable firm. Her dedication to staying updated and her proactive approach to filling her employment gap impressed her employer. Emma's story highlights the importance of staying engaged with your industry and leveraging volunteer opportunities to maintain and enhance your skills.

Story 4: Michael's Overcoming Health Challenges to Find Employment

Background

Michael, a software developer, faced a significant health challenge that required him to take a year-long break from work. During this time, he underwent treatment and focused on his recovery. As he regained his health, Michael was determined to return to his career but felt uncertain about how to address his employment gap.

Strategies Employed

1. **Continuous Learning**: While recovering, Michael kept his mind active by taking online courses in new programming languages and software development

methodologies. This helped him stay current with industry trends.

2. **Freelance Projects**: Michael took on freelance software development projects that he could manage on his own schedule. This allowed him to gradually transition back into work and demonstrate his capabilities to potential employers.

3. **Health and Wellness Focus**: Michael prioritized his physical and mental well-being by maintaining a balanced diet, exercising regularly, and practicing mindfulness. This holistic approach to health enabled him to build resilience and confidence.

4. **Networking and Support**: Michael joined online forums and developer communities where he could share his experiences and

seek advice. He also worked with a career counselor who helped him prepare for job interviews and address his health-related employment gap.

Outcome

Michael successfully re-entered the workforce as a software developer at a tech startup. His dedication to continuous learning and his proactive approach to freelance work showcased his skills and determination. Michael's story demonstrates the importance of resilience, self-care, and leveraging support systems during challenging times.

Story 5: Linda's Career Change to Pursue Her Passion

Background

Linda, a corporate lawyer, felt unfulfilled in her career and decided to take a sabbatical to explore her passion for culinary arts. During her year-long break, Linda attended culinary school, traveled to learn about different cuisines, and honed her cooking skills. As her sabbatical came to an end, Linda was determined to transition to a new career in the culinary industry.

Strategies Employed

1. **Skill Building**: Linda immersed herself in culinary education, completing a professional chef certification and gaining hands-on

experience through internships at renowned restaurants.

2. **Networking in a New Industry**: Linda joined culinary associations, attended food festivals, and participated in cooking competitions. These activities helped her build connections and gain visibility in the culinary community.

3. **Building a Brand**: Linda created a food blog and social media profiles where she shared recipes, cooking tips, and culinary experiences. This online presence showcased her expertise and passion for food.

4. **Leveraging Transferable Skills**: Linda highlighted the transferable skills she gained as a lawyer, such as attention to detail, project management, and communication.

She emphasized how these skills could benefit her in the culinary industry.

Outcome

Linda successfully transitioned to a new career as a chef and opened her own restaurant. Her dedication to skill-building, networking, and personal branding helped her gain recognition and attract customers. Linda's story illustrates the potential for a successful career change when pursuing one's passion and leveraging transferable skills.

Story 6: David's Overcoming Age Discrimination to Secure Employment

Background

David, an experienced sales manager in his mid-50s, faced a prolonged period of unemployment after his company was acquired and his position was eliminated. Despite his extensive experience, David struggled to find a new job, suspecting that age discrimination played a role in the rejections he received. Determined not to let his age define his job prospects, David adopted a proactive and strategic approach to his job search.

Strategies Employed

1. **Modernizing Skills**: David enrolled in online courses to update his skills, particularly in digital marketing and data analytics, which

were increasingly important in his field. This demonstrated his commitment to staying current with industry trends.

2. **Revamping Resume and LinkedIn Profile**: David worked with a career coach to revamp his resume and LinkedIn profile, highlighting his achievements and downplaying dates that might reveal his age. He focused on his results-driven approach and the value he brought to previous employers.

3. **Networking Across Generations**: David expanded his network by joining industry groups and attending networking events where professionals of all ages gathered. He reached out to younger colleagues and mentors to

learn from their experiences and share his own.

4. **Targeted Job Applications**: David targeted companies known for their inclusive hiring practices and those that valued experience and mentorship. He tailored his applications to emphasize how his extensive experience could benefit these organizations.

Outcome

David successfully secured a role as a senior sales consultant at a progressive tech company that valued diversity and experience. His ability to adapt to new technologies and his extensive industry knowledge made him a valuable asset. David's story highlights the importance of continuous learning, effective personal branding, and strategic networking in overcoming age-related challenges in the job market.

Story 7: Maria's Overcoming Cultural Barriers to Find a Job

Background
Maria, an immigrant with a background in engineering, faced significant cultural and language barriers when she moved to a new country. Despite her qualifications and experience, she struggled to find a job due to these challenges. Determined to succeed, Maria focused on building her language skills and adapting to the new work culture.

Strategies Employed
1. **Language Improvement**: Maria enrolled in intensive language courses to improve her proficiency. She practiced speaking with native speakers and participated in

language exchange programs to enhance her communication skills.

2. **Cultural Adaptation**: Maria attended workshops and seminars on workplace culture and professional etiquette in her new country. She also sought advice from colleagues and mentors who had successfully navigated similar challenges.

3. **Volunteering and Internships**: To gain local experience and build her network, Maria volunteered for engineering projects and took on internships. These opportunities allowed her to apply her skills in a new context and gain valuable references.

4. **Professional Networking**: Maria joined professional associations and attended industry events to connect

with other engineers and potential employers. She actively participated in networking sessions and sought out mentorship opportunities.

Outcome

Maria's dedication to improving her language skills and understanding the local work culture paid off. She secured a position as a project engineer at a reputable engineering firm. Her persistence and willingness to adapt demonstrated her commitment and capability. Maria's story underscores the importance of language proficiency, cultural adaptation, and leveraging volunteer opportunities to overcome barriers in the job market.

Story 8: Robert's Journey from Addiction to Career Success

Background

Robert, a talented graphic designer, struggled with addiction, which led to a significant gap in his employment history. After seeking help and achieving sobriety, Robert was determined to rebuild his career. He faced the dual challenge of overcoming the stigma of addiction and proving his readiness to return to the workforce.

Strategies Employed

1. **Recovery and Rehabilitation**: Robert focused on his recovery by participating in a rehabilitation program and attending support groups. Achieving and maintaining sobriety was his top priority.

2. **Skill Refreshment**: To regain his confidence and update his skills, Robert enrolled in graphic design courses. He also completed certifications in new design software and techniques.
3. **Building a Portfolio**: Robert created a new portfolio showcasing his recent work, freelance projects, and personal design initiatives. He used this portfolio to demonstrate his creativity and technical proficiency.
4. **Open and Honest Communication**: During interviews, Robert addressed his employment gap openly and honestly. He emphasized his recovery journey, the steps he had taken to achieve sobriety, and his

commitment to maintaining a healthy lifestyle.

5. **Support from Mentors and Networks**: Robert sought guidance from mentors who had experience in the graphic design industry. He also joined online design communities to connect with other professionals and seek advice.

Outcome

Robert successfully re-entered the workforce as a graphic designer at a creative agency. His honesty, dedication to recovery, and updated skill set impressed his employer. Robert's story highlights the importance of resilience, continuous learning, and transparent communication in overcoming personal challenges and achieving career success.

Story 9: Lisa's Overcoming Long-Term Caregiving Responsibilities

Background

Lisa, an experienced healthcare administrator, took an extended break from her career to care for her elderly parents. After several years of full-time caregiving, Lisa was ready to return to work but faced challenges related to her employment gap and the perception that she might not be up-to-date with industry developments.

Strategies Employed

1. **Online Learning and Certifications**: Lisa enrolled in online courses and earned certifications in healthcare administration, patient care, and healthcare technology. This

demonstrated her commitment to staying current with industry trends.

2. **Volunteer Work in Healthcare**: Lisa volunteered at a local hospital, assisting with administrative tasks and patient care. This allowed her to gain recent experience and fill her employment gap with relevant work.

3. **Resume and Cover Letter Updates**: With the help of a career coach, Lisa updated her resume and cover letter to highlight her caregiving experience as a period of skill-building and personal growth. She emphasized the transferable skills she gained, such as time management, organization, and empathy.

4. **Professional Networking**: Lisa reconnected with former colleagues and attended healthcare industry conferences and networking events. She joined professional associations to stay informed about industry developments and connect with potential employers.

Outcome

Lisa successfully re-entered the workforce as a healthcare administrator at a reputable medical center. Her dedication to continuous learning, volunteer work, and strategic networking helped her overcome the challenges of her employment gap. Lisa's story illustrates the importance of leveraging caregiving experiences, staying current with industry trends, and building a strong professional network.

Story 10: Ben's Overcoming Legal Issues to Rebuild His Career

Background

Ben, a construction project manager, faced legal issues that led to a brief period of incarceration and a significant gap in his employment history. Determined to rebuild his career, Ben focused on addressing the challenges posed by his legal history and demonstrating his commitment to personal and professional growth.

Strategies Employed

1. **Legal Resolution and Rehabilitation**: Ben worked closely with legal advisors to resolve his legal issues and comply with all requirements. He also participated in rehabilitation programs to

address any underlying issues and demonstrate his commitment to personal growth.

2. **Skill Enhancement**: During his time away from formal employment, Ben took online courses in construction management, project planning, and safety regulations. He earned certifications that enhanced his qualifications.

3. **Building a Strong Support Network**: Ben connected with mentors and support groups who provided guidance and encouragement. He sought advice from professionals who had successfully navigated similar challenges.

4. **Honest Communication**: In job applications and interviews, Ben

addressed his legal history openly and honestly. He focused on his rehabilitation, the steps he had taken to improve himself, and his readiness to contribute positively to the workforce.

5. **Freelance and Contract Work**: To gain recent experience and build his reputation, Ben took on freelance and contract construction management projects. He successfully completed these projects and received positive feedback from clients.

Outcome

Ben successfully re-entered the workforce as a construction project manager at a reputable construction firm. His commitment to personal growth, continuous learning, and honest communication impressed his employer. Ben's story highlights the importance of resilience, transparency, and leveraging support networks to overcome significant personal challenges and rebuild a successful career.

Conclusion

These real-life success stories demonstrate that overcoming employment gaps and finding meaningful employment is achievable with the right strategies, mindset, and support. Each individual's journey is unique, but common themes of continuous learning, networking, volunteering, and resilience emerge as key factors in their success. By drawing inspiration from these stories and applying similar strategies, you can navigate the challenges of unemployment and achieve your career goals.

Your Path to Career Triumph: Final Thoughts

Navigating the job market after a period of unemployment can be a daunting and emotional journey. Whether you've faced layoffs, health challenges, caregiving responsibilities, or any other reason for your employment gap, this book aims to provide you with the tools, strategies, and inspiration needed to overcome these challenges and achieve your career goals. In this concluding chapter, we will summarize the key takeaways from the book, reinforce the importance of a positive mindset, and offer final words of encouragement as you embark on your journey to career success.

Key Takeaways

Throughout this book, we've explored various strategies and practical advice to help you re-enter the workforce and land the job of your dreams. Here are the key takeaways from each chapter:

Chapter 1: Understanding Employment Gaps
- Employment gaps are common and can occur for various reasons, such as layoffs, health issues, and family responsibilities.
- Employers may have concerns about employment gaps, but understanding these concerns can help you address them effectively.
- Reframing employment gaps as periods of growth and development

can change perspectives and reduce stigma.

Chapter 2: Overcoming the Stigma of Employment Gaps

- Changing perspectives on employment gaps involves being honest and transparent about your experiences.
- Highlighting relevant activities, such as volunteering, freelancing, and skill development, can turn gaps into strengths.
- Confidence and proactive strategies are essential in addressing employer concerns and shifting the hiring conversation.

Chapter 3: Strategies for Re-Entering the Workforce

- Networking is a powerful tool for discovering job opportunities and gaining support from peers and mentors.
- Leveraging social media, volunteering, and freelancing can help you stay engaged and build a strong professional network.
- Building a personal brand and showcasing your work through a portfolio can enhance your visibility and credibility.

Chapter 4: Crafting Your Winning Resume

- Highlighting your strengths, using creative formatting, and turning employment gaps into positives are

key to creating a compelling resume.
- Functional and hybrid resume formats can de-emphasize employment gaps and focus on your skills and accomplishments.
- Providing strong references and focusing on transferable skills can strengthen your job applications.

Chapter 5: Acing the Interview
- Thorough preparation, including researching the company and practicing common interview questions, is essential for interview success.
- Addressing employment gaps confidently and positively can mitigate employer concerns.
- Making a strong impression involves dressing appropriately, showing

enthusiasm, building rapport, and following up with a thank-you email.

Chapter 6: Mindset and Mental Health
- Managing anxiety and depression, focusing on your strengths, and setting realistic goals are crucial for maintaining a positive mindset.
- Building confidence through self-care, positive self-talk, and practicing interview skills can enhance your job search experience.
- Staying connected with a support system and celebrating small wins can help you stay motivated and resilient.

Chapter 7: Daily Routines for Success
- Establishing effective daily routines and maintaining a healthy lifestyle

are essential for productivity and well-being.
- Creating structure through morning rituals, daily planning, and end-of-day reflection can help you stay organized and focused.
- Prioritizing physical and mental health, using productivity tools, and taking breaks can boost your overall performance.

Chapter 8: Continuous Learning and Skill Development

- Embracing continuous learning and skill development is crucial for staying competitive and achieving long-term career success.
- Utilizing resources such as online courses, workshops, books, and mentorship programs can enhance your skills and knowledge.

- Integrating learning into your daily routine and applying new skills in real-life scenarios can reinforce your growth and adaptability.

Chapter 9: Real-Life Success Stories
- Real-life success stories demonstrate that overcoming employment gaps and finding meaningful employment is achievable with the right strategies, mindset, and support.
- Common themes of continuous learning, networking, volunteering, and resilience emerge as key factors in these success stories.
- Drawing inspiration from these stories and applying similar strategies can help you navigate the challenges of unemployment and achieve your career goals.

Embracing a Growth Mindset

A growth mindset is the belief that abilities and intelligence can be developed through dedication and hard work. Embracing this mindset is crucial for overcoming employment gaps and achieving career success. Here are some final thoughts on cultivating a growth mindset:

1. Embrace Challenges
- View challenges as opportunities to learn and grow. Instead of avoiding difficult situations, face them with determination and curiosity.
- Remember that setbacks and failures are part of the learning process. Each obstacle you overcome strengthens your resilience and skills.

2. Learn Continuously

- Commit to lifelong learning and self-improvement. Stay curious and open to new experiences, knowledge, and perspectives.
- Seek out opportunities to learn, whether through formal education, on-the-job training, or self-directed study.

3. Persevere Through Difficulties

- Stay persistent and maintain a positive attitude, even when faced with challenges or rejection. Your determination will pay off in the long run.
- Use setbacks as motivation to work harder and smarter. Reflect on what you can learn from each experience and how you can improve.

4. Celebrate Progress

- Acknowledge and celebrate your progress, no matter how small. Recognize your achievements and use them as motivation to keep moving forward.
- Set realistic goals and milestones, and take pride in reaching them. Each step you take brings you closer to your ultimate career goals.

Final Words of Encouragement

As you embark on your journey to re-enter the workforce and achieve your career goals, remember that you are not alone. Many others have faced similar challenges and successfully overcome them. With the right strategies, mindset, and support, you can navigate the job market with confidence and resilience.

Believe in Yourself: Trust in your abilities and the value you bring to potential employers. Your experiences, skills, and unique perspective are your strengths.

Stay Positive and Persistent: Maintain a positive outlook and stay persistent in your efforts. The job search process can be challenging, but your determination and resilience will lead to success.

Seek Support: Reach out to friends, family, mentors, and professional networks for support and guidance. Surround yourself with positive influences who encourage and uplift you.

Celebrate Your Journey: Embrace the journey of self-discovery, growth, and achievement. Each step you take, no matter how small, is a testament to your strength and determination.

In closing, remember that your career journey is unique and full of potential. By applying the strategies and insights from this book, you can overcome employment gaps, build a fulfilling career, and achieve your dreams. Here's to your success and the exciting opportunities that lie ahead!

Appendices

Appendix A: Sample Resumes and Cover Letters

Sample Resume 1: Chronological Format

Jane Doe
jane.doe@example.com | LinkedIn: [linkedin.com/in/janedoe](https://www.linkedin.com/in/janedoe) | +123-456-7890

Professional Summary:
Results-driven marketing professional with over five years of experience in developing and executing successful marketing campaigns. Proven ability to increase brand awareness and drive sales through strategic planning and innovative techniques.

Key Skills:

- Project Management
- Digital Marketing
- Communication
- Data Analysis
- Leadership

Professional Experience:

Marketing Manager

XYZ Company, New York, NY

January 2018 – Present

- Developed and executed comprehensive marketing strategies that increased brand awareness by 40%.
- Managed a team of 10 marketing professionals, providing mentorship and guidance to achieve departmental goals.
- Coordinated cross-functional teams to deliver successful product launches, resulting in a 20% increase in sales.

Marketing Specialist
ABC Corporation, New York, NY
June 2015 – December 2017

- Designed and implemented marketing campaigns that boosted customer engagement by 30%.
- Collaborated with the sales team to develop targeted marketing materials, contributing to a 15% increase in lead generation.

Education and Certifications:
- Bachelor of Science in Marketing, University of New York
- Digital Marketing Certification, Google
- Project Management Professional (PMP) Certification

Sample Cover Letter

[Your Name]
[Your Address]
[City, State, ZIP Code]
[Your Email Address]
[Your Phone Number]
[Date]

[Employer's Name]
[Company's Name]
[Company's Address]
[City, State, ZIP Code]

Dear [Employer's Name],

I am writing to express my interest in the Marketing Manager position at [Company's Name], as advertised on [where you found the job listing]. With over five years of experience in developing and executing successful marketing campaigns, I am confident in my ability to contribute to your team and help [Company's Name] achieve its marketing goals.

In my previous role as Marketing Manager at XYZ Company, I successfully increased brand awareness by 40% through the development and execution of comprehensive marketing strategies. I also managed a team of 10 marketing professionals, providing mentorship and guidance to achieve departmental goals. My ability to coordinate cross-functional teams resulted in a 20% increase in sales from successful product launches.

I am particularly impressed by [Company's Name]'s commitment to innovation and customer satisfaction. I am excited about the opportunity to bring my expertise in digital marketing, project management, and data analysis to your team and contribute to the continued success of [Company's Name].

Thank you for considering my application. I look forward to the opportunity to discuss how my skills and experiences align with the needs of your team. Please feel free to contact me at [your phone number] or [your email address] to schedule an interview.

Sincerely,
[Your Name]

Sample Resume 2: Functional Format

John Doe

john.doe@example.com | LinkedIn: [linkedin.com/in/johndoe](https://www.linkedin.com/in/johndoe) | +123-456-7890

Professional Summary:
Dynamic and results-oriented IT professional with a proven track record in system administration and technical support. Adept at managing complex IT projects, troubleshooting issues, and implementing innovative solutions to enhance system performance.

Key Skills:
- System Administration
- Technical Support
- Network Security
- Project Management
- Troubleshooting

Professional Experience:

System Administrator (Freelance)

January 2020 – Present

- Managed the installation, configuration, and maintenance of servers and network infrastructure for multiple clients.
- Implemented security protocols and performed regular system audits to ensure data integrity and compliance with industry standards.
- Provided technical support to clients, resolving issues promptly and efficiently.

IT Support Specialist

XYZ Corporation, New York, NY

June 2015 – December 2019

- Provided technical support to over 200 employees, resolving hardware and software issues.

- Managed IT projects, including system upgrades and network installations, ensuring minimal downtime and disruption.

- Developed and implemented IT policies and procedures to enhance system security and efficiency.

Education and Certifications:

- Bachelor of Science in Information Technology, University of New York
- CompTIA Network+ Certification
- Certified Information Systems Security Professional (CISSP)

Sample Cover Letter

[Your Name]
[Your Address]
[City, State, ZIP Code]
[Your Email Address]
[Your Phone Number]
[Date]

[Employer's Name]
[Company's Name]
[Company's Address]
[City, State, ZIP Code]

Dear [Employer's Name],

I am excited to apply for the IT Support Specialist position at [Company's Name], as advertised on [where you found the job listing]. With a strong background in system administration and technical support, I am confident in my ability to provide exceptional IT support and contribute to the success of [Company's Name].

In my previous role as an IT Support Specialist at XYZ Corporation, I provided technical support to over 200 employees, resolving hardware and software issues efficiently. I also managed IT projects, including system upgrades and network installations, ensuring minimal downtime and disruption. My ability to develop and implement IT policies and procedures enhanced system security and efficiency.

I am particularly impressed by [Company's Name]'s commitment to leveraging technology to drive innovation and improve business processes. I am eager to bring my expertise in system administration, technical support, and project management to your team and contribute to the continued success of [Company's Name].

Thank you for considering my application. I look forward to the opportunity to discuss how my skills and experiences align with the needs of your team. Please feel free to contact me at [your phone number] or [your email address] to schedule an interview.

Sincerely,
[Your Name]

Appendix B: Helpful Resources

1. Job Search Websites
- **Indeed**: A comprehensive job search engine that aggregates job listings from various sources, including company websites, job boards, and recruitment agencies.
- **LinkedIn Jobs**: A powerful platform for job searching and networking. Utilize LinkedIn to connect with industry professionals and apply for job openings.
- **Glassdoor**: Offers job listings, company reviews, salary information, and interview insights to help you make informed career decisions.
- **Monster**: A well-established job search website that offers job

listings, resume advice, and career resources.

2. Networking Platforms

- **LinkedIn**: The leading professional networking platform for connecting with colleagues, industry professionals, and potential employers.
- **Meetup**: A platform for finding and attending local networking events, industry meetups, and professional gatherings.
- **XING**: A professional networking platform popular in Europe, particularly in German-speaking countries.

3. Online Learning Platforms

- **Coursera**: Offers online courses and certifications from top universities and institutions on a wide range of subjects.

- **edX**: Provides access to online courses and programs from renowned universities and organizations.
- **LinkedIn Learning**: Offers a vast library of video tutorials and courses on business, technology, creative skills, and personal development.
- **Udemy**: Features a wide variety of courses on diverse topics, taught by industry experts.

4. **Career Development Resources**
- **CareerOneStop**: Sponsored by the U.S. Department of Labor, this resource offers job search tools, career exploration resources, and resume writing tips.

- **The Muse**: Provides career advice, company profiles, and job listings to help you find and navigate your career path.
- **Idealist**: A platform that connects job seekers with opportunities in the non-profit sector, including jobs, internships, and volunteer positions.

5. Mental Health and Wellness Support

- **BetterHelp**: An online platform that offers access to licensed therapists and counselors for mental health support.
- **7 Cups**: Provides online therapy and emotional support from trained listeners and licensed professionals.
- **National Alliance on Mental Illness (NAMI)**: Offers resources,

support groups, and information on mental health conditions and treatment options.

Appendix C: Interview Preparation Tools

1. Practice Interview Questions
- **Big Interview**: An online platform that offers video-based interview practice, coaching, and feedback to help you prepare for interviews.
- **Mock Interview Practice**: Schedule mock interviews with friends, mentors, or career coaches to simulate real interview scenarios and receive constructive feedback.

2. Interview Preparation Checklists
- **Pre-Interview Research**: Create a checklist to ensure you research the company, understand the job description, and prepare questions for the interviewer.

- **Interview Day Essentials**: Prepare a checklist of items to bring to the interview, such as multiple copies of your resume, a list of references, a notepad, and a pen.

3. Body Language Tips

- **Positive Body Language**: Practice maintaining good posture, making eye contact, and using appropriate hand gestures to convey confidence and engagement during the interview.
- **Relaxation Techniques**: Learn relaxation techniques, such as deep breathing and visualization, to calm your nerves before and during the interview.

Appendix D: Sample Interview Questions and Answers

1. Tell Me About Yourself

Answer Example:

"I am a dedicated marketing professional with over five years of experience in developing and executing successful marketing campaigns. I have a proven track record of increasing brand awareness and driving sales through strategic planning and innovative techniques. In my previous role as a Marketing Manager at XYZ Company, I managed a team of 10 marketing professionals and led cross-functional teams to deliver successful product launches. I am passionate about leveraging my skills to contribute to the

growth and success of [Company's Name]."

2. Why Do You Want to Work Here?

Answer Example:

"I am excited about the opportunity to join [Company's Name] because of its reputation for innovation and commitment to excellence. I have always admired [Company's Name]'s approach to [specific aspect of the company or industry], and I believe my skills and experiences align well with the company's goals. Additionally, I am impressed by [Company's Name]'s dedication to employee development and community involvement. I am eager to contribute to the company's success and be part of a dynamic team."

3. What Are Your Strengths and Weaknesses?

Answer Example (Strengths):

"One of my key strengths is my ability to manage complex projects efficiently. In my previous role, I successfully led a marketing campaign that resulted in a 30% increase in sales. I am also highly adaptable and thrive in fast-paced environments. My strong communication skills enable me to build positive relationships with clients and colleagues."

Answer Example (Weaknesses):

"One area I am working on improving is my delegation skills. I tend to take on too many tasks myself, which can lead to burnout. To address this, I have been focusing on building trust with my team and delegating responsibilities more

effectively. This has allowed me to manage my workload better and empower my team members."

4. Describe a Challenge You've Faced and How You Overcame It

Answer Example:

"At my previous job, our team faced a significant challenge when we lost a major client due to budget cuts. This resulted in a loss of revenue and morale. I took the initiative to lead a strategy session with my team to identify new business opportunities. We developed a targeted marketing campaign to attract new clients and re-engage existing ones. Through our efforts, we secured three new clients within six months, which helped us recover the lost revenue and boost team morale."

5. Where Do You See Yourself in Five Years?

Answer Example:

"In five years, I see myself taking on greater leadership responsibilities within [Company's Name]. I am committed to continuous learning and professional development, and I aspire to advance to a senior management position where I can contribute to the company's strategic goals. I am particularly interested in [specific area of interest], and I hope to lead initiatives that drive innovation and growth in this area."

Appendix E: Resource List

Job Boards and Career Websites
-Indeed: www.indeed.com
-LinkedIn Jobs: www.linkedin.com/jobs
- Glassdoor: www.glassdoor.com
- Monster: www.monster.com

Networking and Professional Associations
- LinkedIn: www.linkedin.com

- Meetup: www.meetup.com
- XING: www.xing.com
- Professional Associations: www.directoryofassociations.com/

Online Learning Platforms
- Coursera: www.coursera.org
- edX: www.edx.org
- LinkedIn Learning: www.linkedin.com/learning
- Udemy: www.udemy.com

Career Development Resources

- CareerOneStop: www.careeronestop.org
- The Muse: www.themuse.com
- Idealist: www.idealist.org

Mental Health and Wellness Support

- BetterHelp: www.betterhelp.com
- 7 Cups: www.7cups.com
- National Alliance on Mental Illness (NAMI): www.nami.org

UK Job Search Resources

1. **Find a Job - GOV.UK**:
   www.gov.uk/find-a-job
   Find a job - Search and apply for jobs in England, Scotland, and Wales.
2. **Indeed UK**: uk.indeed.com
   Indeed UK - Search millions of jobs online.
3. **WikiJob**: www.wikijob.co.uk
   Best Job Sites in the UK - A list of the top job boards in the UK.
4. **National Careers Service**: Job Vacancies - Find job vacancies and get career advice.
5. **JobHelp**: Job Search Advice - Get job search advice, CV tips, and support from employers and work coaches.

UK Mental Health Support Websites

1. **Mind**: www.mind.org.uk
2. **Mental Health Foundation**: www.mentalhealth.org.uk

Canada Job Search Resources

1. **Job Bank**: Job Bank - Search job postings and explore career planning tools.
2. **Indeed Canada**: Indeed Canada - Search millions of jobs from thousands of job boards.
3. **Workforce Canada**: Find a Job - Search for jobs and get career advice.
4. **LinkedIn Canada**: Job Search - Find job opportunities and connect with employers.
5. **CareerOneStop**: Career Resources - Explore career planning and job search resources.

Canada Mental Health Support Websites

1. **Canadian Mental Health Association (CMHA)**: www.cmha.ca
2. **Wellness Together Canada**: www.wellnesstogether.ca

Australia Job Search Resources

1. **SEEK**: SEEK - Australia's number one job site.
2. **Indeed Australia**: Indeed Australia - Search millions of jobs online.
3. **Workforce Australia**: Find a Job - Search for jobs and get career advice.
4. **LinkedIn Australia**: Job Search - Find job opportunities and connect with employers.
5. **JobSearch Australia**: Job Search - Search for job vacancies and get career advice.

Australia Mental Health Support Websites

1. **Beyond Blue**:
   www.beyondblue.org.au
2. **Headspace**: www.headspace.org.au

Final Note

This Appendices section is designed to provide you with additional tools and resources to support your job search journey. The sample resumes and cover letters offer templates to guide you in crafting compelling applications, while the interview preparation tools and sample questions aim to help you present yourself confidently and effectively. Utilize the resource list to explore job boards, networking platforms, online learning opportunities, and career development support.

Remember, the journey to finding meaningful employment is unique for each individual. Stay persistent, remain positive, and continue to seek opportunities for growth and improvement. With the right mindset and strategies, you can overcome employment gaps and achieve your career aspirations.